HYPOALLER ENIC CATS

BUYER'S GUIDE

ALL THE FACTS AND INFORMATION YOU
NEED CHOOSING A HYPOALLERGENIC CAT.
INCLUDES PROFILES ON ALL FOURTEEN
LOW-ALLERGY CAT BREEDS.

BY
TIM ANDERSON

Copyright Information

Table of Contents

INTRODUCTION

There are large numbers of cat lovers all over the world. However, some can't have a feline companion in their homes because they, a spouse, partner, or child is allergic to cats. For many of these people, a much better option than no cat is to get a hypoallergenic cat.

Cats can cause allergies in two ways: the dander from their coats and the protein contained in their saliva and in the oils secreted from their skin. Some allergic reactions to cats can be very severe and range from asthma and other breathing problems to skin conditions that are painful, itchy, and / or unsightly.

Fortunately for cat lovers with an allergy problem, there are some cat breeds that don't cause reactions that are as severe or any allergic reactions at all! In fact, there are now no fewer than 14 hypoallergenic cat breeds to choose from to suit all tastes, homes, and lifestyles.

This book looks at the difference between "hypoallergenic" and "non-allergic" and the causes of allergic reactions to cats, and it provides a list of the top hypoallergenic breeds. In addition, it offers a profile of each of these 14 breeds in terms of their history, temperaments, health considerations, and the overall advantages and disadvantages of the breed. There is also advice on how to further reduce allergens in your home.

The overall aim of this book, therefore, is to allow cat lovers who suffer from allergies to still enjoy the company of cats without the sneezing, itching, wheezing, and so forth. It offers guidance about the best breed to fit your lifestyle and home and helpful information and tips.

However, it is very important to please note that no breed is 100% hypoallergenic for *all* individuals! One still *must* spend some time with a cat before bringing it home to make sure it doesn't trigger a reaction.

CHAPTER 1: WHAT IS MEANT BY HYPOALLERGENIC?

What is meant by non-allergenic?

If something is non-allergenic, it means, quite simply, that it does not cause an allergic reaction at all. When it comes to pets, and cats in particular, there is unfortunately no such thing as a non-allergenic breed.

There are, however, some breeds that are the next best thing to non-allergenic: they are hypoallergenic.

What is meant by hypoallergenic?

Hypoallergenic does *not* mean that there will be no allergic reaction. What it does mean, though, is that there is either very little likelihood of an allergic reaction or that any reaction that is experienced will be minor or at least easy to manage.

The good news for those who love cats but are allergic to them is that there are now 14 different hypoallergenic cat breeds to choose from! However, because each person is different and will therefore respond differently to each breed, it is *essential* for an allergy sufferer to arrange with a breeder to spend time with a kitten or cat to assess their reaction to it before buying it and taking it home.

It must be kept in mind that a breed that one person can live with easily and without any adverse reaction might cause allergies to varying degrees or intensity in somebody else.

What makes a cat allergenic?

Contrary to popular belief, it is not cat hair itself that is the allergen. There are two closely connected causes of allergies that are experienced by some people in relation to cats.

The first allergen is dander (no, not dandruff). This substance consists of tiny or microscopic pieces of dried skin. These come loose from the skin and float in the air and settle on bedding, furniture, and on people's skin and clothes. These tiny particles are even smaller than dust mites, so they are certainly not visible with the human eye.

These minute pieces of skin would not cause any problems at all if it weren't for the glycoprotein Fel d1, which is produced in the sebaceous or oil glands in the cat's skin. The protein is also found, albeit to a lesser extent, in cats' saliva and their urine. This means that there is Fel d1 on cats' hair or coats firstly because cats lick themselves during grooming and as a result of the oils the skin secretes as part of keeping the coat healthy.

Significantly, there is more Fel d1 produced by some breeds than others. In addition, unsterilized cats produce more of this glycoprotein than cats that have been either spayed or neutered. In addition, unneutered male cats produce higher levels of Fel d1 than both neutered males and female cats. A general rule of thumb may therefore be that a spayed, female cat will produce less Fel d1 than other female cats or male cats.

Those people who are unfortunate enough to suffer from cat allergies can be affected in different ways and to varying degrees:

> ➤ If the dander that carries some Fel d1 is inhaled through the nose, it can cause hay fever, which manifests itself as sneezing, a running nose, and / or an itchy nose. Dander that is inhaled into the nose can also lead to a chronic condition called allergic rhinitis. This causes the same

symptoms as hay fever but can also lead to nasal and sinus congestion and an accompanying post-nasal drip, which in turn can cause a sore or irritated throat or even a cough.

➢ If the dander particles are breathed into the nose and mouth and reach the lungs and the bronchial tubes, asthma attacks can result in those who are prone to asthma or who have lungs that are weak or vulnerable. If severe enough, asthma poses a very serious and frightening health risk as it makes breathing very difficult. Less severe reactions include a persistent cough or even some wheezing.

➢ Skin rashes can result from dander or shed hairs landing on the skin, as a result of petting a cat, or after being licked by one. These are usually very mild reactions. However, those who suffer from Atopic dermatitis (Eczema) may find their condition becomes worse after contact with a cat.

➢ Dander that gets onto the face or into the eyes can cause itching and redness of the eyes.

CHAPTER 2: CHOOSING THE RIGHT HYPOALLERGENIC BREED

What to look for

When one selects a cat – any cat – it is important to spend time with it before one takes it home. This is even more important if one is looking for a cat that is hypoallergenic. If the allergy sufferer doesn't spend time around the breed first, then he or she may only discover that they are reacting badly once the new kitten or cat has been introduced into the home. Having to return a cat is difficult for the people involved and very traumatic and unsettling for the cat.

One needs to arrange to go to the breeder's premises and sit in a room or enclosed area with the cats. If the allergy sufferer feels fine after being with the cats for an hour or so, then it's time to go to stage 2: stroking or petting the cats. If all is still well, one can then proceed to stage 3 and pick up a kitten or cat.

When it comes to selecting an individual cat, one could keep in mind that generally females of all cat breeds produce lower levels of the problem-causing protein Fel d1 than males do. It might be, therefore, that getting a female is usually a better bet for allergy sufferers.

It is very important to remember that there may be some reaction, even with a hypoallergenic cat. As indicated earlier, no cat is non-allergenic.

What one is hoping and aiming for is no allergic reaction or a very mild adverse reaction that one can deal with and manage with ease!

Finding the best breed for your lifestyle

Choosing the breed is as important as choosing the individual cat once you have settled on the breed. One mustn't be swayed by price, looks, or the cuteness factor.

Assuming there have been no problematic allergic reactions when the allergy sufferer spent time with a specific breed, there are a number of other factors that one must take into account when selecting a breed:

- ✓ **Personality or temperament**: Do you want an affectionate cat that is demanding, even clingy? Do you want a cat that is loving and loyal but still independent? Do you prefer quiet, aloof cats? Are you looking for a doting lap cat? Is intelligence and trainability important in the breed? In other words, you need to select a breed that will be a good fit for you in terms of your wants, needs, and your own personality.

- ✓ **Grooming needs**: Are you willing to devote time daily or weekly to grooming a cat? Are you prepared to do some things that may not always be pleasant but that some breeds need from an owner in order to stay in good condition and healthy? If you don't have the time and/or the inclination, you must avoid grooming-intensive or high maintenance breeds.

- ✓ **Time requirements**: Part of needing time to devote to a cat is, of course, for grooming. However, other breeds need a lot of time from their owners because they need attention and cuddles. Others are high-energy cats that are intelligent and require exercise and stimulation. If you are away a lot and don't have time for grooming, cuddling, and/or playing, you probably shouldn't get any kind of cat!

✓ **Sociability**: Do you have children? Are there dogs or other cats in your home? If the answer to these questions is "Yes," you need to look for a breed that is sociable or good with children and that will get along with – or at least not be in conflict with – other cats and cat-friendly dogs.

✓ **Energy or activity levels**: If you don't have time, energy, or space, it is perhaps not a good idea to get a breed that needs lots of space, play, and stimulation. If the cat needs one or all of these things and doesn't get them, it will be unhappy, even depressed, and may become 'naughty' out of sheer boredom.

So, it's important to know what the nature and needs of a breed are in order to make sure that you and the breed are a good match or fit!

A list of suitable breeds per main characteristic can be found at the end of chapter 3. This 'list' of primary features may help you make a decision if you are undecided or torn between several breeds.

List of the top 14 hypoallergenic cat breeds

There is now an amazing selection of cat breeds available that are, to varying degrees, hypoallergenic. Remember, though, that no cat is non-allergenic.

There is a debate about which breeds can accurately be considered hypoallergenic. Some critics say that there is not nearly enough scientific evidence about levels of Fel d1 and dander in various breeds. Others believe that the wealth of anecdotal evidence gives clear indications of which breeds are far less likely to cause allergic reactions in humans.

However, despite the debates and disagreements, there seems to be an overall consensus that the following breeds are options for those who suffer from cat allergies:

1. The Siberian
2. The Balinese
3. The Javanese
4. The Bengal
5. The Cornish Rex
6. The Devon Rex
7. The LaPerm
8. The Oriental Shorthair
9. The Russian Blue
10. The Ocicat
11. The Burmese
12. The Color-point Shorthair
13. The Siamese
14. The Canadian Sphynx.

The next chapter will provide descriptions and images of each of these breeds so that you have enough basic information to decide which cats you want to learn more about and/or meet.

In addition, keep in mind that just because most cats in breed X are demanding doesn't mean that all of them will be. As with people, there are always individual differences. If you want some sort of indication of what a kitten's temperament might be, meeting his or her mother can be helpful. Often kittens' personalities are influenced by their mothers.

CHAPTER 3: THE HYPOALLERGENIC BREEDS

The Siberian

The Siberian, also known as the Siberian Forest Cat and occasionally the Moscow Semi-Longhair, tops several of the hypoallergenic lists, as it is reportedly the least likely breed to cause problems for its owners.

This is thanks to the fact that these cats produce far less Fel d1 than cats of most other breeds. There have been some scientific studies done with this breed that confirms this. The Siberian is also a natural rather than an 'engineered' breed, the national cat of Russia, charming, and very beautiful!

History of the breed

With the Siberian, there are no stories about breeders who were inventive, pioneering, or just plain lucky as these cats evolved naturally. As a result, it is impossible to say exactly when the breed emerged. However, mention of these cats is found in regional and other Russian folktales that are centuries old.

Their name arises from the fact that they were first encountered in Siberia in Russian. This forested region with its freezing winters and very heavy snows is no doubt responsible for the breed's thick, long, and dense coat. Once domesticated, they were initially valued by their owners because of their hardiness and hunting prowess. They kept vermin of various kinds away from houses, farms, grain, other valuable stores, and from businesses.

Despite their very long histories, Siberians were not seen outside of Russia until very recently. In fact, the first Siberians were only imported into America in 1990! The International Cat Association (TICA) recognized the breed in 1996 followed by the American Cat Fanciers Association (ACFA) in 1999. In 2006, the Cat Fanciers Association (CFA) also registered the breed. However, the color-point Siberian is known as the Neva Masquerade by some registries such as Europe's Feline Federation.

Breed's temperament

Siberian cats make wonderful pets and companions for single people of all ages, families, and both experienced and first-time cat owners. They are affectionate, active, playful, and very intelligent cats.

Their warm, loving, and sociable natures make the Siberian ideal in homes where there are children, other cats, and cat-friendly dogs. These cats are easy-going and relaxed, and not much bothers them or makes them anxious. In fact, their calmness makes them an ideal choice as therapy cats. They are also often found keeping an owner or family member company when he or she is under the weather.

They are also intelligent, curious, and bold, and they enjoy poking about in cupboards, boxes, or packets to see what interesting things might be in them. A Siberian will welcome the chance to play games that challenge it mentally, are interactive, and give it a chance to use its athletic and agile body and hunting skills. Games that involve stalking, chasing, and pouncing are ideal. Because of their intelligence, they are easy to train and are eager to learn tricks.

The breed's origins in the Siberian wilds are responsible both for its hunting prowess and its enjoyment of games and activities involving water. For instance, it will enjoy splashing and being splashed during an owner's bath time and might also bat at the water in its bowl with a paw.

They are very loving, affectionate, and loyal cats who take a keen and genuine interest in their owner or family. They enjoy human companionship so they will pad around after their person and 'help' while they do things around the house and garden. The Siberian loves cuddles and curling up on a lap and will be greet you enthusiastically when you get home.

They enjoy communicating with their owner and do so using a range of sweet sounds: occasional soft meows, trills, chirps, and lots of loud purring. However, despite their loving and affectionate temperaments, they are not needy or demanding. They are happy to be in your company and wait until you have time for a game or cuddles.

Appearance

As with some other breeds, Siberians are found in a wide range of colors and patterns either with or without white. However, in the case of the Siberian, any and every color is genetically possible. Coat markings include color-point, tortoiseshell (tortie), solid, and tabby. In other words, unlike with other breeds, there is no breed-specific color or pattern / markings.

These cats have broad heads in keeping with their stocky bodies and very sweet, gentle expressions. The ears are medium to large. Tufts of fur are found in the ears (and between their toes). The eyes of a white Siberian are often blue or may even be odd colors. Other colors or patterns may have copper, green, gold, or a mixture such as green-gold.

The Siberian is a medium- to large-sized cat and are slow to mature. They only reach their full adult weight after 5 years. Adult cats usually weigh anything between 8 and 17 lbs. or 3.5 to 7.5kg. Female cats weigh about 25% less than their male counterparts. This breed can exceed this weight range at times.

In addition, the long, thick coat; fluffy plume-like tail; muscular build; barrel chest; thick ruff around the neck; thickly furred britches; and large, round, and tufted paws often make these splendid cats look larger than they actually are!

Needs of the breed

In addition to those that all cats have (food, shelter, love, and medical care), the Siberian has modest needs. The primary requirements of the breed are cuddles and companionship, play time, and conversation.

However, they are not clingy or overly demanding cats. The Siberian will quietly wait until its owner has time for them. After waiting patiently, it will seize an opportunity for a cuddle or a game with great enthusiasm, purring throughout.

Their coats are easy to care for despite its length. A bi-weekly brush will keep their fur healthy and free of dead hair. Like all cats, they do require regular nail clipping, occasional ear cleans, and daily—or at least weekly—dental care to avoid periodontal or gum disease.

Health

Generally speaking, a Siberian will live for up to 16 years with the correct care and nutrition. Some individual cats may exceed this period. This is a hardy and healthy breed overall. This is in large part thanks to the fact that it is a natural breed rather than one that has been engineered.

However, they are a little more prone to hypertrophic cardiomyopathy, which is a condition that results in an enlarged heart muscle, than some other breeds. Although this is a serious and incurable disease, it can be managed and controlled.

There are several prescribed medicines that are used to treat hypertrophic cardiomyopathy. Cats with this cardiac illness must be under the care of a vet so that they can be monitored regularly and given the required medication. With the right care and an early diagnosis, these cats can live good and happy lives for many years.

Owners can help to manage hypertrophic cardiomyopathy too. A Siberian that is affected by this condition must be on a controlled diet in order to keep both its weight and blood pressure down. Being overweight and having raised blood pressure place additional strain on a heart that already has to work harder than it should. In addition, cats with this problem should be protected from too much excitement, strenuous activity, or stress. Fortunately, their sweet, laid-back natures make this easier than it otherwise might be. Their medical condition will make them less active than their healthy counterparts are.

Pros and cons

The levels of Fel d1 protein found in Siberians is, in most cases, far lower than in other breeds. It is important to note, though, that Fel d1 *is* still present. In addition, the common and popular silver Siberians produce more Fel d1 than other colors. Fortunately, that still leaves a dazzling range of colors from which to choose.

The grooming required by these cats is on par with most breeds; although because they have a triple coat, brushing is required twice rather than once a week. On the upside, these cats usually love being brushed and cooperate fully! Barring unforeseen events, a Siberian should not need to be bathed. If they do, though, the fact that they like water does make giving these playful cats a bath much less difficult, fraught, and hazardous than it otherwise might be.

Price range

The Siberian is far from inexpensive because they are still not easy to come by. At time of writing, the price range was $700 to $1400 or £450 to £900.

The Balinese

History of the breed

The only aspect of the history of the Balinese that is not in dispute is the fact that it is not from Bali! One theory is that this breed is a natural or spontaneous longhaired mutation of the Siamese. The support for this theory lies in the fact that longhaired kittens are reported to have appeared in litters along with their shorthaired siblings since the early 1900s. A second theory is that the gene that is responsible for long hair was introduced into Siamese bloodlines after World War I when breeders at the time tried to rejuvenate faltering lines after the war had all but stopped all breeding programs. There is not enough support on either side to declare a winner; both theories are feasible.

The ancestors of theses cats were Siamese imported from Thailand to America and the UK in the mid 1800s. The first Balinese outside of Thailand resulted from a breeding program that worked to preserve the recessive long-haired gene in this first Siamese breeding pool. This breed was not formally or seriously bred until 1955. A woman in California, USA by the name of

Marion Dorsey of *Rai-Mar Cattery* began breeding the longer-haired Siamese. In the 1960s, Dorsey was joined by Helen Smith from *MerryMews Cattery* in New York, USA. The breed's distinctive flowing coat is reportedly responsible for its name as it reminded Smith of the robes of graceful, traditional dancers of Bali. In 1965, Dorsey sold her cattery to Sylvia Holland who continued to breed the Balinese.

The earliest recognition of the breed was by the American Cat Fanciers Federation (CFF) who registered them as "Long-haired Siamese" in 1928.

It was the 1950s that saw a drive to get these cats recognized as a distinct breed. It was established that when a Balinese was bred to another Balinese, the kittens were always, well, Balinese. This proved that it is a 'pure breed' rather than a mutation of the Siamese.

The breed standard was subsequently developed by Sylvia Holland in the 1960s and 1970s. The Balinese standards are based on the modern or more contemporary Siamese build: slender, elongated bodies, and a distinctive wedge-shaped head.

Breed's temperament

The Balinese shares its temperament with its ancestor, the Siamese. These are very intelligent, alert, social, and playful cats. They are also very vocal, but their voices are not as loud or 'raspy' as those of the Siamese.

They are also extremely loving and affectionate cats that adore time with their owners and playing energetic games. They are very acrobatic and energetic and love to entertain their people even if it is at the expense of their own dignity. As the Cat Fanciers Association (CFA) website puts it, "Despite his regal bearing and aristocratic appearance, the Balinese is a clown with a heart as big as a circus tent."

Appearance

One of the distinctive characteristics of the Balinese is the coat that flows rather than lying close to the sleek, elegant body. The hair itself is silky and soft to the touch. A further distinctive feature is the fact that there is no fluffy undercoat as there is in most long-haired cats. The tail is plume-like thanks to the long, flowing hair.

Like other cats with a point pattern, Balinese kittens are white or cream at birth. As they get older, they slowly develop color or points on the face, tail, ears, and paws. Interestingly, Balinese in cool or colder climates are darker than their counterparts in the warmer parts of the world. Eye color varies and the intensity of the color can be affected slightly by the point color, the individual cat's age, and—oddly—by diet.

The majority of cat associations accept the Balinese in seal, cream, blue, chocolate, and lilac points. Lynx points and tortoiseshell in all of these colors are also accepted. However, the Cat Fanciers Association (CFA) only accepts the breed in the classic seal, chocolate, lilac, and blue points.

As with the Siamese, there are two body types. The first is the modern shape or type (pictured above). These cats are graceful and slender and have fine bones, elongated bodies, wedged-shaped heads, broad ears, and a long tapering muzzle. The traditional body shape has a broader head and a more sturdy body. Both types have long legs and tails, almond-shaped eyes, and neat oval paws.

Needs of the breed

In addition to those that all cats have (food, shelter, love, and medical care), the Balinese has fairly modest needs. The primary requirements of the breed are cuddles, companionship, play time, and conversation. However, they are not clingy or overly demanding cats.

Their coats are easy to care for despite its length. A weekly brush will keep their silky fur healthy and free of dead hair. These affectionate cats quite often enjoy grooming sessions, which makes it easier. Like all cats, they do require regular nail clipping, occasional ear cleans, and daily—or at least weekly—dental care to avoid periodontal disease.

Health

This breed is healthy and robust generally. However, it does share a few genetic illnesses or defects thanks to the Siamese heritage.

The first is the potential for crossed or partially crossed eyes. They are also genetically predisposed to gingivitis or gum disease and to amyloidosis, which destroys the liver. With amyloidosis, a fibrous protein called amyloid is deposited in the liver. These deposits disrupt the normal functioning of the organ. There is no cure for amyloidosis, but supportive care is very helpful.

With the correct nutrition and care, these lovely cats have a very long lifespan of 18 to 22 years.

Pros and cons

There is a great deal of anecdotal evidence that indicates that the Balinese causes very few and only mild allergic reactions. Although there haven't been many scientific tests done, those that have been carried out indicate that the breed produces less Fel d1 and Fel d2 proteins than the majority of cat breeds. In addition, the minimal shedding means less dander is likely to float about in the air.

Price range

At time of writing, the price range for a Balinese was $500 to $3000 for a show cat or breeding quality or £320 to £1925.

The Javanese

History of the breed

Just as the Javanese is not from Bali, the Javanese is not from Java. Like many others, the breed originated in America and was named in the 1950s by Helen Smith, who was one of the original breeders. Like the Balinese, the Javanese is also derived from the Siamese. The other breeds in the Siamese-style group are the Oriental Short- and Long-hair and the Color-point Shorthair.

This is where it gets a little complicated. Because all of these breeds share a general body type and have very similar personalities, the main distinguishing features are coat, colors, and markings. The Siamese comes in pointed colors: chocolate, seal, lilac, and blue. The Balinese comes in the same colors, but it is long haired. The Javanese comes in cream, red, tortoiseshell, and lynx points and is long haired. The Color-point Shorthair comes in the same colors as the Javanese but is short-haired.

The picture as far as breed recognition is concerned is also a little confusing. The International Cat Association (TICA) lists the Balinese as a championship breed but does not recognize the Javanese as a separate breed. The Cat Fanciers Association (CFA) recognized the breed in 1987. However, in 2008, they decided that the Javanese is actually a division of the Balinese breed.

Breed's temperament

In terms of temperament, the Javanese is similar to the Siamese and Balinese in many respects. They are intelligent, curious, sociable, active, loving, and very chatty. They are very good with children and get along well with other cats and cat-friendly dogs.

The Javanese is an ideal breed for people who want a cat that is very interactive and loves to keep their owner company. They are extremely affectionate and loyal and are lap cats that will also—given half a chance—sleep on or even in the bed with their person at night. Their enjoyment of and need for company and interaction means that these cats become unhappy, even depressed, if left on their own for too long and often. However, owners of the Javanese say they are not as demanding as the Siamese.

Because of their intelligence, desire to please, and love of play, these cats are easy to train. The Javanese will play fetch and can be trained to walk on a leash and do tricks. In fact, because of their quick brains, they need entertainment and stimulation in the form of games or toys they can play with on their own. A bored Javanese may decide to 'kill' the toilet roll or 'rearrange' the furnishings.

Appearance

The standards in terms of appearance for the Javanese are almost the same as for the Balinese, Siamese, Oriental Longhair, Color-point Shorthair, and the Oriental Shorthair. The significant differences are hair length and colors.

This medium-sized breed has a sleek, muscular body and long, slim-boned legs. The weight range for adult Javanese is 5 to 10 lbs. or 2.25 to 4.5kg. Their hind legs are a little longer than the front legs.

The head is triangular in shape and tapers to a point. The ears are large, pointed at the tip, and wide at the base. Like the Siamese and Balinese, the eyes are almond-shaped. Eye color varies depending on coat color. These cats have small, oval paws, and the tail is thin and tapers to a point.

The coat is medium length, fine, soft, and silky. As with the Balinese, the tail hair is the longest and the tail itself looks rather like a flowing plume, especially when these cats run. The point colors found in the Javanese include cream, lynx point, color-point, tortoiseshell point, and red. Also, these cats are found in parti-colors such as lilac-cream or tortoiseshell-chocolate.

Needs of the breed

The grooming required by these cats is on par with most breeds, and it is only necessary to brush them once a week. In fact, given that the coat is medium in length and soft and silky in texture, the coat doesn't tangle and is therefore easy to care for. Also, barring unforeseen events, a Javanese should not need to be bathed.

As with all cats, their nails need clipping from time to time and their teeth must be cleaned daily or at least weekly to prevent periodontal or gum disease.

Health

This breed is healthy and robust generally. However, it does share a few genetic illnesses or defects thanks to the Siamese heritage.

The first is the potential for crossed or partially crossed eyes. They are also genetically predisposed to gingivitis or gum disease and to amyloidosis, which destroys the liver. With amyloidosis, a fibrous protein called amyloid is deposited in the liver. These deposits disrupt the normal functioning of the organ. There is no cure for amyloidosis, but supportive care is very helpful.

With the correct nutrition and care, the Javanese will live for 12 to 15 years.

Pros and cons

The downside with the Javanese is firstly that they are very talkative even if their voices are not as loud as the Siamese's. So, if you want a cat that is quiet, docile, independent, and calm, this is not the breed for you.

They also need a lot of interaction and playtime, so if you can't give this, you should perhaps consider a less needy and active breed. Finally, as these cats like to follow their owner around, they can get a little underfoot. This can be a problem and a danger for an older or less steady owner.

Price range

At time of writing, the price range for a Javanese was $500 to $1200 for a show cat or breeding quality or £320 to £770.

The Bengal

History of the breed

The Bengal is not a natural breed. It is a hybrid of the domestic cat and the Asian Leopard Cat. In other words, these cats contain some 'wild' DNA. The development of this breed began as recently as the 1970s and the name is derived from the Leopard Cat's scientific name, _Felis Bengalensis_, not from the Bengal Tiger as some people think.

The beginnings of the Bengal are to be found in the laboratory where Dr. Willard Centerwall was doing research on Leukemia. He was interested in the Leopard Cat because it is immune to feline Leukemia. He theorized that these wild cats may therefore hold the key to a cure for this form of cancer in both cats and humans.

It was in this scientific and medically orientated context that the cross between the Leopard Cat and a domestic cat first took place. In the 1980s, Dr. Centerwall became ill and as a result was winding down his research program. A breeder by the name of Jean Sugden (now Jean Mill) acquired several Leopard Cat hybrids from him. These cats were the ancestors of the domestic Bengal and the original breeding stock.

Jean Mill had several goals. The first was to produce a cat breed that had a 'wild' look but the temperament of a domestic cat. Secondly, she wanted to create a domestic cat that had a beautiful coat in the hopes that it would discourage people from buying and using fur garments.

In addition to Mill, the other significant early breeders were Greg and Elizabeth Kent. They produced Bengals by crossing Egyptian Maus with their Leopard Cat. Mill bred female cats to the Kent's Leopard cat too. In fact, the Kent breeding line is still considered one of the purest Bengal bloodlines.

The breed rapidly gained in popularity thanks to the cat's unique looks. The International Cat Association (TICA) recognized the Bengal in 1987 and ranks it as one of the most popular breeds. Conversely, the Cat Fanciers Association (CFA) doesn't even recognize it as a separate breed!

Breed's temperament

The Bengal today is many generations from its partly wild heritage and is a wonderful domestic breed. They may not be lap cats, but that doesn't mean they aren't very affectionate, loving, and loyal. They enjoy human company and love playing active games, especially those that involve chasing, stalking, and pouncing and so mimics the hunting activities that, like their wild ancestors, they are so good at.

These very energetic, alert, and agile cats love activity including swimming or messing about in water. A Bengal is likely to join its owner in the bath or shower. They are jumpers that enjoy—and are very good at—climbing onto high surfaces such as bookshelves and the tops of refrigerators and doors. Their energy level and intelligence means that they are quick to learn how to open doors and windows. This skill can pose a challenge for owners who don't want their cat getting into or out of rooms or cupboards. They learn tricks, play fetch, and will walk on a leash.

They are also very vocal cats, and their voices are fairly loud and hard to ignore. However, even though they are a bit of a handful and rather 'loud,' they are immensely fun, lively cats that are ideal for a household in which there are children who will be playmates.

Appearance

In most cases, what one notices first about the Bengal is its unique, beautiful coat that is spotted or marbled / tri-colored. Some cats also glitter or seem to shine in the light thanks to the structure of the hair shaft. Those who have a chance, and are fortunate enough, to pet a Bengal also discover that the coat feels as good as it looks as it is extremely soft and very dense.

The markings of the Bengal resemble the spots of a Leopard. They are found in two different patterns: marbled or rosettes that form a half circle. In either case, the spots should be in sharp contrast to the background color of the coat. The rosettes are the result of what is known as tri-coloring where there is a dark outline with lighter colors within the line.

There is a wide range of colors, and The International Cat Association (TICA) recognizes 13. These colors include blue, snow (white), brown, silver, charcoal, black (melanistic), chocolate, cinnamon, seal lynx point, seal sepia, tabby, and seal mink. With the exception of the black or melanistic Bengal, the breed standard requires that the tummy is white or light colored.

In terms of general build, the Bengal is a muscular, sleek, athletic cat that is usually medium to large in size. On average, adult male cats weigh 10 – 15 lbs. (4.5 – 6.8kg) and the females 8 – 12 lbs. (3.6 – 5.4 kg).

The head is wedge-shaped and both it and the muzzle are broad. The cheekbones are high, and the ears are smaller than in many breeds with rounded tips. The eyes are round and wide with dark markings around them that rather resemble eye makeup or mascara. The back or hind legs are a little longer than the front legs, and this gives these cats a slight arch to their backs when they are standing. This stance is yet another feature that contributes to its 'wild' look.

Needs of the breed

Because they are such very active and lively cats, they need space, stimulation, and lots of playtime.

The grooming required is minimal with a weekly brush being more than sufficient. Barring unforeseen events, a Bengal does not need to be bathed. However, if it does, it is not a chore or traumatic for the cat or the owner as it will love every minute of being in the water! As with all cats, their nails need clipping from time to time, and their teeth must be cleaned daily or at least weekly to prevent periodontal or gum disease.

Health

One of the benefits of a hybrid cat or breed is that it is usually very hardy and far less prone to genetic illnesses or disorders.

There is an extremely small chance of hypertrophic cardiomyopathy, which is a genetic condition that results in an enlarged heart muscle. Although this is a serious, incurable disease, it can be controlled. There are several medicines that are used. These cats must be under the care of a vet for regular monitoring. With the right care, these cats can live good and happy lives for many years.

Owners can help to manage hypertrophic cardiomyopathy too. A Bengal that is affected by this condition must be on a controlled diet in order to keep both its weight and blood pressure down. In addition, cats with this problem should be protected from too much excitement, strenuous activity, or stress. Fortunately, their sweet, laid-back natures make this easier than it otherwise might be. Their medical condition will make them less active than their healthy counterparts are.

The Bengal may also suffer from chronic anemia. This means that there are fewer red blood cells than is necessary in order to carry oxygen to the tissues. However, the majority of cats live healthy and long lives. Early diagnosis improves the prognosis. Depending on the type of anemia, treatment varies and usually involves supplements, and blood transfusions are only necessary in severe cases.

With love, enough exercise, and the correct nutrition, the Bengal will live for 12 to 18 years.

Pros and cons

These cats are great fun to have around the house and wonderful playmates for children. However, they are not for everyone because they demand—often very loudly and persistently—attention. Bengals can be a handful, so it is not the best breed for a first-time cat owner. Someone wanting a quiet and well-behaved lap cat should not get a Bengal as they are busy and may even 'steal' and hide objects, especially shiny ones, they take a fancy to.

As with any cat, a zero allergic reaction is not guaranteed, although anecdotal evidence strongly suggests that many individuals who normally react badly to cats are fine around the Bengal.

Price range

At time of writing, the price range for a Balinese was $400 to $900 or £260 to £580.

The Cornish Rex

History of the breed

The Cornish Rex is a natural mutation. The first kitten appeared in a litter of barn cats that were born in 1950 in Cornwall, England. This first Cornish Rex was given the unusual name of Kallibunker by the farmer's daughter. The kitten was covered in tiny, tight curls. With his cream coat, he apparently looked like a miniature lamb.

As Kallibunker grew and matured, other unique features became evident. He was slender, had long legs, very large bat-like ears, a narrow head, and a long, thin tail. The name "Cornish Rex" was a result of the similarity between the cat's coat and the coat of the curly-haired Rex rabbit that is found in that part of Cornwall, UK.

When it was realized that this cat was a true mutation, he was bred back to his mother, and two curly kittens were produced. They in turn were crossed with British domestic shorthairs, Siamese, and Burmese in order to strengthen and widen the UK's breeding program's genetic pool.

The breeding program in America used one of Kallibunker's offspring and outcrossed to Havana Browns and American Shorthairs in addition to domestic shorthairs, Siamese, and Burmese. As a result of various careful breeding programs, the gene pool for this breed is now very strong. As a result, outcrossing is no longer required or allowed.

The Cornish Rex was recognized by the Cat Fanciers Association (CFA) in 1964. The International Cat Association (TICA) and the American Cat Fanciers Association (ACFA) also accept the breed at championship level.

Breed's temperament

This breed is ideal if you want a cat that adores its owner, playing games, showing off, and food. If, however, you want a quiet, docile cat, then don't consider the bouncy Cornish Rex.

These highly intelligent cats are curious, even nosey, alert, and like to explore their environments. They are quick to learn tricks, will play fetch, and are ideal for agility training. Games that are very active and involve jumping, running, and climbing are their favorites. The Cornish Rex stays playful and kittenish well into its adult years.

Their sociability and intelligence make them highly adaptable, so they cope with moving house and travel far better than most breeds. They also get along very well with other cats and with cat-friendly dogs. They really love human company and are warm, affectionate, purring lap cats. They are also very loyal cats who are attached to their owners and want to share his or her life, space, and activities.

Be warned, though, that they also love food—including yours—and they are not above stealing some in the kitchen or from your plate if you aren't vigilant at meal times and don't put food away where your cat can't get to it!

Appearance

The Cornish Rex is a cat that is characterized by waves, curls, and curves. It has an arched body, a curly coat, and large but rounded ears. Without a doubt, the most striking feature of the breed is the coat thanks to both its look and feel. Some describe the fur as feeling like lamb's wool, others liken it to rabbit fur, and there are those who say it feels like cut velvet. The coat's softness is due to the fact that the coat consists of a down layer or undercoat only.

These fun-loving and acrobatic cats look very aristocratic with their high cheekbones, hollow cheeks, strong chins, and high-bridged noses. The ears are very large for the smallish egg-shaped head. Their eyes are large, oval in shape, and expressive. Eye colors include blue, green, aqua, amber, copper, yellow, gold, hazel, or orange. Some cats also have odd eyes.

The Cornish Rex has a slim waist, a barrel chest, and thin, long legs. They may look fragile and only weigh on average 6 to 10 lbs. or 2.7 to 4.4kg, but they are actually muscular and hard-bodied, which is what gives them their remarkable athletic and acrobatic skills. It also means that they usually feel heavier than they look.

The Cornish Rex comes in a wide range of colors and patterns that are also accepted by the various associations for judging purposes. Firstly, there are the solid colors: orange, black, white, and chocolate. These cats are also found in the tabby range of ticked, mackerel, and classic tabby. In addition, there are creams, lilacs, blues, greys, bi-colors, tortoiseshell, and color-point.

Needs of the breed

Because of their playful, active, and loving natures, these cats need space and a lot of attention. They require games, conversation, playtime, and cuddles… and lots of it. If you live in a very small home and/or are away from home often, your

Cornish Rex will not be a happy, well-adjusted cat. An animal companion will help to ease the loneliness, however.

These cats are very easy to take care of from the grooming perspective as none is needed. In fact, brushing is discouraged as it can damage the curly coat.

As with all cats, their nails need clipping from time to time and their teeth must be cleaned daily or at least weekly to prevent periodontal or gum disease.

Health

These hardy cats are not prone to any breed-specific illnesses or conditions. The only medical caution is in relation to anesthetics as all the Rex breeds have a slight tendency to react very badly to them. Milder forms of anesthesia are therefore recommended wherever possible. A veterinarian will use the appropriate caution in this regard.

With the necessary care, the Cornish Rex lives for 14 to 18 years.

Pros and cons

The Cornish Rex produces as much of the allergenic protein Fel d1 as any other breed. However, many allergy sufferers have these cats because they shed very little and the hairs are short. This means there is less dander. Anecdotal evidence indicates that this breed causes fewer allergy-related problems.

These cats are not suitable for small homes or where they will be left alone a great deal as they need space and companionship. Without these things, these cats are prone to become depressed and even 'naughty' from boredom or unhappiness.

Finally, because they only have an undercoat, the Cornish Rex feels the cold more than many other breeds. This might mean increased heating costs if you live in a cold place.

Price range

At time of writing, the price range for a Cornish Rex was $350 to $700 or £225 to £450.

The Devon Rex

History of the breed

Like the Cornish Rex, the Devon Rex is a natural mutation that
was first discovered in the UK in the 1960s. A woman by the
name of Beryl Cox found a stray cat that gave birth to a litter
shortly thereafter. One of the kittens had curly hair. Beryl Cox
named the elf-like kitten Kirlee, and he was the ancestor for all
Devon Rexes that followed.

Initially, it was thought that Kirlee was a Cornish Rex. However,
this was disproved when breeders tried to produce kittens using
Kirlee and female Cornish Rexes. It was then realized that Kirlee
and the Cornish Rex were distinct breeds. Once this had been
established, and the genes responsible for the breed's looks had
been identified, a breeding program ensured that the Devon Rex
cats went from strength to strength.

The breed gained recognition with various cat associations very
rapidly with most giving the Devon Rex full status in the late
1960s. The Cat Fanciers Association (CFA) initially only
recognized it as a subgroup within the Rex category. However,
1978 saw the breed being granted full status by the CFA.

Breed's temperament

Some describe the Devon Rex as the ultimate companion pet because it is such a loving, outgoing, loyal, fun, energetic, and affectionate cat. They are also very intelligent and are able—and in fact keen—to learn a range of tricks and desirable behaviors. These cats are also ideal for agility training, playing fetch, and can be taught to walk on a leash and even walk to heel.

The Devon Rex adores their person. They will greet you on your return home, follow you around, and keep you company while you bathe, cook, clean, watch television, work, etc. Although it is not a chatty cat and its quiet voice is rarely heard, it has a purr that can drown out conversation when it is in full flow!

Their love of their person and athletic ability combine to produce a behavior that is typical of most of the Devon Rexes: they will climb or leap onto their person's shoulder and lie or sit there parrot-like for as long as they are allowed to remain there. They may also choose to drape themselves behind their owner's neck like a short fur stole. These are not cats that are concerned about elegance, dignity, or appearances. Their priorities are closeness, affection, comfort, and fun. They are also dedicated lap cats when a shoulder is not available and will share their person's bed given half a chance.

Although they adore human company and playing games, they are also perfect cats for those people who work during the day as the Devon Rex is good at staying out of trouble and entertaining itself. The only behavior that can be trying is that they are a little prone to beg at meal times. Like the Cornish Rex, the Devon Rex loves food. These cats may even steal food from the kitchen or even off a plate if their owner is not careful and vigilant. However, if this behavior is discouraged when the cat is young, it can be stopped or prevented.

Appearance

The appearance of the Devon Rex has been likened to that of aliens, pixies, and elves. Certainly they look like no other cat with their huge ears; long, thin neck; short muzzle; uniquely shaped head; high cheekbones; and their large, intense eyes.

They are medium-sized cats that weigh on average 6 to 9 lbs. or 2.7 to 4kg. The females weigh a little less than the males. Their build is slender yet muscular with long, slightly bowed front legs, and this adds to their quirky appearance. They also have small feet but larger than normal toes that allow the Devon Rex to pick things up in a way other cats can't.

The coat differs from cat to cat with some having the typical Rex curls or ripples and others with a coat that looks and feels more like suede or down. In terms of the breed standards, all colors and markings are acceptable. Common colors include solids, tabby, pointed, shaded, smoke, and bi-color. The Devon Rex cats that have Siamese pointed coloring are called Si Rex rather than Devon Rex.

The eye colors should match the coat or hair color. Odd eyes, for example one blue and one brown or amber eye, are not uncommon in the breed, especially with white cats.

Needs of the breed

The primary needs of the Devon Rex are love, cuddles, and play time. In terms of grooming they are not hard work. However, because the coat is not thick or straight and the hairs are delicate, rough or frequent brushing can actually cause breakage and damage.

If a Devon Rex starts to feel a little greasy, they will not put up too much of a struggle in the bath and are real wash-and-go cats thanks to the thin coat!

As with all cats, their nails need clipping from time to time and their teeth must be cleaned daily or at least weekly to prevent periodontal or gum disease.

Health

Generally, this is a very healthy and robust breed, but these cats can be susceptible to a few genetic conditions. The two serious ones are hypertrophic cardiomyopathy and hereditary myopathy.

Hypertrophic cardiomyopathy is a condition that results in an enlarged heart muscle. Although this is a serious and incurable disease, it can be managed and controlled with medication, diet, and by keeping the cat relaxed, at ideal weight, and not exercising it too much. With the right care and an early diagnosis, these cats can live good and happy lives for many years.

Hereditary myopathy is a central nervous illness that affects muscle function and control, rather like cerebral palsy. With this condition, there is no treatment, and only supportive care can be given. The disease is usually stable or slowly progressive. The course of the disease will depend on the severity of the myopathy.

A less serious genetic condition is patellar luxation where the kneecap pops out of place causing a limp and some pain. Often, it will also spontaneously pop back in, but in more serious cases, surgery is required. This can be a once-off, recurring, or a chronic condition.

If one buys a cat from a reputable breeder, he or she should have scanned the breeding pair for these conditions. The breeder should also provide a written health guarantee in terms of these conditions with each Devon Rex kitten.

Pros and cons

The Devon Rex produces as much of the allergenic protein, Fel d1, as any other breed. However, some allergy sufferers have these cats because the hairs are short and they shed less than some, which can reduce the amount of dander. As with any breed, though, an allergy sufferer must be exposed to a cat to assess reaction before taking a new cat home.

This breed is ideal for families with children and other pets because of its sociable, outgoing, and playful nature. These cats also travel well and make very good therapy cats.

While the Devon Rex is low maintenance when it comes to grooming, the hairs and whiskers are a little prone to breakage. While the hair and whiskers will grow back, the whiskers won't reach the usual or previous length.

Price range

At time of writing, the price range for a Devon Rex was $700 to $1200 or £450 to £770.

The LaPerm

History of the breed

The first LaPerm was also a natural mutation and, like the Cornish Rex, born to a barn cat. The original LaPerm kitten was born in Oregon in America in 1982. Unlike its mother and five siblings, this kitten was completely bald at birth. However, its skin bore a pattern or shadow of classic tabby markings. During the first eight weeks of its life, this little bald cat underwent an astonishing transformation as it grew a full coat of very curly and soft hair. It was given the appropriate name of Curly.

The owner of this cat, Linda Koehl, assumed that Curly was a once-off or a fluke of nature. There was therefore no thought of breeding with Curly. What changed this state of affairs was the fact that over the course of the next decade, there was an increase of bald kittens and curly-haired cats on the farm. This prompted Koehl to discuss the situation with a local vet. Once she had a better understanding of genetics, and it was confirmed that these cats were not either Cornish or Devon Rexes, controlled breeding began in earnest. The breed was named LaPerm because of the curly coat.

The reaction to the breed was strong from the first time a LaPerm appeared in a cat show. People were both interested in and excited by this beautiful new type of cat, and the demand for them was almost immediate, very strong, and steady. The LaPerm was recognized and granted full championship status by The International Cat Association (TICA) in 2002. The Cat Fanciers Association (CFA) also recognizes the breed.

Breed's temperament

These cats are wonderful pets and companions, including for families with children who know how to handle and interact with cats. The LaPerm is active, playful, gentle, inquisitive, and are very loving and affectionate. However, it is not a clingy or overly demanding cat.

Their sociable natures also make them a good choice for homes with cat-friendly dogs. Their gentleness and playfulness means that they are excellent companions for children who treat them with respect. Their intelligence allows them to learn tricks with ease and to enjoy interactive and more challenging games and toys. This intelligence also combines with their playful, inquisitive natures and their dexterous paws to produce a cat that will work out how to open cupboards and doors. Owners of LaPerms sometimes have to take steps to keep their cats out of places they don't want them to get into.

While LaPerms rarely use their quiet voices, they are experts at purring. The purr is usually most noticeable when he or she is on a lap or a shoulder, being petted, when their owner or a family member talks to him or her, or when these sweet cats gently pat a shoulder to indicate they are there or pat a face to remind their person that they are loved.

Although these cats seek out human company, they will wait patiently for attention if their owner is busy with something else.

The LaPerm will be content to be in the same room but won't need to be asked twice to jump onto a lap.

Appearance

The LaPerm is sometimes bald or shorthaired at birth and, like Curly, acquires its striking curly coat as it gets older. Other kittens are born with short or wavy hair that they then lose before getting their adult or mature coats. Interestingly, a LaPerm kitten's pedigree includes the letters BC, BB, or BS. These letters indicate whether the kitten was born curly, bald, or straight. A very small number of kittens don't develop the characteristic curly coat, but this is rare.

The nature of the curls can be loose or tight curls, ringlets, or even corkscrew-like curls. The curls are at their tightest on the tummy, the throat, and at the bases of the ears. Cats with longer hair can also have ruffs around their necks and a rather splendid plumed tail. The long whiskers are often curly too.

These cats are found in every possible color and pattern. However, tabby and tortoiseshell are the most common markings or patterns. The coat itself is fairly soft to the touch, although it varies a little depending on the hair length and tightness of the curls. The hair fairly often parts naturally down the center or middle of the back.

The LaPerm only reaches maturity at two or three years old. Adult cats weigh 5 to 10 lbs. or 2.25 to 4.5 kg on average. Females weigh slightly less than the males. They are muscular, medium-sized cats and should not be either stocky or long and slim.

The head is wedged-shaped but has rounded contours and a flat forehead. The muzzle is full and the nose is broad but moderate in length. The ears are also of medium size, wide at the base, and have rounded tips. The eyes are medium to large and set fairly far apart. Like the coat, the eyes come in a range of colors and they are almond-shaped, slanting towards the base of the ear.

Needs of the breed

The LaPerm needs playtime, love, and cuddles more than anything else. This is naturally in addition to the nutrition and medical care all cats require.

These cats are easy to groom and only need a brush once or twice a week to prevent tangles or matting in their curls. Fortunately, they enjoy the attention. A comb or brush with revolving teeth is best as it will not straighten the curls or break the hair. If a bath is ever required, a LaPerm should be patted or rubbed gently with a towel and air dried. Vigorous toweling may damage the coat, and blow-drying will give it a frizzy coat!

As with all cats, their nails need clipping from time to time, and their teeth must be cleaned daily or at least weekly to prevent periodontal or gum disease.

Health

This natural breed is generally healthy and robust and not known to suffer from any specific genetic illnesses or conditions. Of course, like all cats, it is necessary to have vaccinations and de-worming done when necessary.

The average life expectancy is 12 to 16 years.

Pros and cons

The LaPerm produces as much of the allergenic protein, Fel d1, as any other breed. However, some allergy sufferers have these cats because they shed less. As with any breed, though, an allergy sufferer must be exposed to a cat to assess reaction before taking it home.

There really is no downside with these cats. They are ideal for families with children and other pets, they are low maintenance in terms of grooming, and they are loving and loyal companions.

Price range

At time of writing, the price range for a LaPerm was $300 to $800 or £190 to £510.

The Oriental Shorthair

History of the breed

The Oriental Shorthair was originally developed in the UK during the 1950s and 1960s. This hybrid initially met with a great deal of resistance from Siamese cat breeders who felt that there was no need or room for yet another oriental cat. However, this new breed rapidly became popular with cat lovers.

This breed was the result of careful crossing of Siamese with Domestic Shorthairs and Russian Blues. In the late 1960s, American breeders modified the breed by crossing Siamese with Domestic Shorthairs and Abyssinians. The intention of both UK and USA breeding programs was to produce the Oriental in as a wide a range of colors and patterns as possible. They were very successful as these cats are now found in more than 300 different combinations of pattern and color!

The Cat Fanciers Association (CFA) recognized the Oriental Shorthair in 1972 with championship status being granted in 1977. In 1985, the breed was accepted by The International Cat Association (TICA).

Breed's temperament

Temperamentally, the Oriental Shorthair and the Siamese are almost identical. Both breeds are very talkative, intelligent, loving, playful, affectionate, and demanding. These are cats that share their owner's lives, homes, beds, etc. They like to be involved and included and don't like being ignored or left alone.

The Oriental Shorthair uses its rough, loud voices to chat to its person and express its views, so if one wants a quiet, docile cat, then this breed is not a good choice. These cats need to be entertained and they must have company. If they don't have something to keep them entertained (an animal companion, puzzle toys, or games) in their owner's absence, they resort to unravelling toilet paper, shredding papers, and various other activities owners really don't want.

Their intelligence and curiosity also means that they will learn to open doors and could end up digging and exploring in places their owner does not really want them to be. They also enjoy climbing into or onto things and scratching around to see what is of interest or worth appropriating for playing with later on.

These are cats that will greet you enthusiastically when you get home, tell you all about their day and enquire about yours, follow you around and 'help' you do things, enter into all activities with energy and enthusiasm, keep you company, and comfort you if you are unwell or unhappy.

Appearance

The Oriental Shorthair is an elegant cat with a slender and long yet muscular body. They move with grace, elegance, and speed. These cats may look delicate, but they are in fact strong and very athletic.

Like all the cats in the Oriental or Siamese group, they have a wedge-shaped head, almond-shaped eyes, and large ears. The medium-sized striking eyes vary in color depending on the coat, and they may be green, blue, or even odd (one green and one blue).

The legs are also slender, and the hind legs are slightly longer than the front legs. The paws, like those of other oriental cats, are small and oval. The tail is thin and tapers to a point.

The coat of the Oriental Shorthair is silky and fine in texture and medium in length. As previously mentioned, these cats are found in an astonishing range of colors and markings or patterns.

The colors include blue, white, ebony or black, chocolate, chestnut, cream, red, lavender, fawn, smokes or the grey range, and cinnamon. Some of the more popular patterns include the solids, tabby, pointed, parti-colored such as tortoiseshell, and bi-color.

Needs of the breed

These cats need attention, love, conversation, stimulation, and activity… and lots of it! If you live in a very small home and/or are away from home, often your Oriental Shorthair will not be a happy, well-adjusted cat. An animal companion and puzzle games will help to ease the loneliness. However, like other active, intelligent breeds, a lonely and bored Oriental Shorthair may act up when left alone.

These cats are very easy to groom. All that is necessary is a weekly combing or brushing to remove dead or loose hair and to keep the coat healthy.

As with all cats, their nails need clipping from time to time, and their teeth must be cleaned daily or at least weekly to prevent periodontal or gum disease.

Health

This breed is susceptible to a few genetic conditions thanks to the Siamese ancestry. The first is crossed or slightly crossed eyes. Secondly, they sometimes have a protrusion of the cranial sternum, but this, like the crossed eyes, is a minor defect that does not impact the cat's well-being or overall health.

A far more serious condition is endocardial fibro elastosis, which is an inflammation of the inner heart muscle. While there is no cure for this illness, it can be managed up to a point. Reputable breeders screen for both this and protrusion of the cranial sternum and will provide a medical clearance certificate.

As a general rule, though, these cats are a robust and healthy breed and live for 12 to 15 years.

Pros and cons

These cats need attention and demand it if they don't get it. They are not a good choice for those who want a quite, docile cat. They are also not a very good combination with other cats that are less active and energetic. They really do not cope with being on their own a great deal and can act up if they feel ignored or left out.

They produce as much Fel d1 protein as any other breed. However, they don't shed very much. As with any breed, though, an allergy sufferer must be exposed to a cat to assess reaction before taking it home.

Price range

At time of writing, the price range for an Oriental Shorthair was $200 to $650 or £130 to £415.

The Russian Blue

History of the breed

The origin of the Russian Blue is unknown, although there are
some colorful theories. The first and more plausible one is that
these cats came from the Archangel Isles in northern Russia and
that they were brought to the UK and Northern Europe in the
1800s by sailors. The second theory—perhaps more a legend than
a theory—is that the breed is descended from the Czars' royal
cats.

What is known is that the breed made its cat show debut at the
Crystal Palace in London, UK in 1875. These cats were initially
known as the "Archangel Cat" and competed in a category with
other blue cats such as the Chartreux from France. The early
1900s saw the breed's arrival in America, and in 1912, the
Russian Blue was shown in its own class.

As was the case with several others, this breed was almost lost during World War II as breeding programs came to a stop. However, later in the 1940s, various breeders began working again to save the Russian Blue and boost the gene pool. In the 1960s, though, breeders in the UK set out to restore these cats to their original appearance, which had been a little lost after some less than ideal crossbreeding. To achieve this, they used the British Blue and Scandinavian cats.

The breeders achieved the look they wanted, but the cat's temperament was problematic in terms of shows because they were very timid and nervous. This caused a decrease in popularity, which continued until the 1980s. As a result of this, breeders began to focus on selective breeding that would address this issue. They also realized that socialization was even more important with Russian Blue kittens than with other breeds as a means of counteracting their natural timidity. These actions have been very successful because only a decade later, the breed was doing very well at shows and was very popular with cat owners. This continues to be the case.

In terms of recognition, the breed was recognized in the U.S. by the Cat Fanciers Association (CFA) in 1949 and later by The International Cat Association (TICA) and the American Cat Fancier's Association (AFCA).

Breed's temperament

The Russian Blue is very affectionate and loving with its family and really enjoys a good game, especially long games of fetch. They are a well-behaved, gentle, and quiet breed with soft voices and a sense of humor. These sensitive cats will also stay with and try to comfort someone who is not well or feeling down.

Russian Blues will greet their owner warmly when he or she gets home, but they also are quite happy to entertain themselves when left alone. They are content to stretch out on a windowsill and watch the world go by, sleep, or just laze about. Although they are usually shy of strangers, they are wonderful companions for adults and children alike. While these cats are affectionate with all family members, they often have a marked preference for one individual.

The Russian Blue is very fastidious when it comes to hygiene and won't use a litter box that is not 100% clean. They also don't cope at all well with change and like routines and a safe, unchanging environment. They are fairly easily startled, and they don't travel well.

Appearance

These are medium-sized, well-muscled, and fine-boned cats. The overall impression is of elegance combined with strength. The double coat is dense and plush, and it makes the Russian Blue look larger than it is.

Russian Blues are, as the name implies, only found in one color. The blue of their coats is a solid color with no patterns or marking. The face is a broad, medium wedge-shape. The forehead is flat, and the profile of these cats is straight and dignified. The ears are large, wide at the base, and placed towards the sides of the head. The coat and eyes are their most striking features.

Interestingly, Russian Blue kittens have yellow eyes. By the time they reach about four months of age, they have developed a bright green ring around the pupil. As the cat matures, the eye color continues to change. A mature cat has bright and vivid green eyes that are round and slightly slanted. Their eyes add to the sweet, innocent, and gentle expression that is so characteristic of this breed.

The coat itself is very dense, and the hairs stick out at 45 degrees to the skin. It is the angle combined with the thickness that makes the coat so luxurious. The Russian Blue's coat is blue, not grey, and often lavender at the base or root of the hair. The tips of the hairs are silver, which gives these cats the appearance of shimmering with reflected light.

Needs of the breed

The Russian Blue loves human company, a good game, having meals served at regular hours, frequent petting and cuddles, and a very clean litter box.

Despite the thickness of the coat, these cats need minimal grooming; a weekly brush is more than adequate to remove loose or dead hair and ensure coat health.

As with all cats, their nails need clipping from time to time, and their teeth must be cleaned daily or at least weekly to prevent periodontal or gum disease.

Health

This is a strong, robust, and healthy breed thanks to the fact that it is a natural breed and, secondly, the care that has gone into the various breeding programs. The only caution is that these cats love their food, and unless owners are disciplined, the Russian Blue can get overweight, even obese, and suffer from all the health problems that go with that.

Pros and cons

This breed is ideal for people who want a gentle, loving, and affectionate cat that enjoys human company but is neither clingy nor demanding. However, they are also easily startled, shy and nervous with strangers, and don't like change.

The Russian Blue produces as much Fel d1 protein as any other breed, but shedding is minimal. As with any breed, though, an allergy sufferer must be exposed to a cat to assess reaction before taking it home.

Price range

At time of writing, the price range for a Russian Blue was $500 to $900 or £320 to £580.

The Ocicat

History of the breed

Despite its appearance and being named for its similarity to the Ocelot, there is no wild DNA in the Ocicat. These cats are the result of formal breeding programs that used Abyssinians, Siamese, and silver tabby American Shorthairs. These genes are responsible for the breed's distinctive coat, bone structure, and very appealing personality.

Like many other breeds, the Ocicat originated in America. The first breeder was a resident of Michigan by the name of Virginia Daly. In 1964, Daly was trying to produce an Abyssinian-pointed Siamese, but the second generation kittens from this program included the desired kittens and a spotted one named Tonga. Daly's daughter called the kitten an 'ocicat' because it resembled and ocelot (the "oci") but was a cat (the "cat" in ocicat). Tonga was considered a once-off and a fluke and was neutered.

However, the same breeding pair produced further spotted kittens with striking copper-colored eyes and ivory coats with golden spots, and Daly made the decision to begin a formal breeding program. Other breeders joined and used the same crossings: Siamese to Abyssinian and the offspring with Siamese. Later on, the American Shorthair was introduced into the breeding program by mistake rather than design. The result was a happy accident though that resulted in an increase in bone size in the Ocicat and the addition of silver to the six existing coat colors.

Tonga was shown at a Cat Fanciers' Association show in 1965, but the breed only achieved full championship status in 1987. The other cat associations followed very soon thereafter. The reason for the long delay was Daly's enforced absence from breeding programs for personal reasons for a period of 11 years. Since the 1980s, the popularity and show presence of the Ocicat has grown by leaps and bounds.

Breed's temperament

The Ocicat is a loving, active, intelligent, chatty, loyal, and sociable breed. They are vocal cats, but they do not talk too much or too loudly.

These cats are fine athletes and very easy to train thanks to their curiosity and intelligence. They will come when called, respond well to basic obedience training, will walk on a leash, fetch, and perform tricks. In fact, a degree of training when they are young will help to prevent them becoming too demanding later on.

They are devoted to their people, good with children, and get along well with other cats and cat-friendly dogs. They enjoy a conversation, are not shy of strangers, and are interested in the activities around them. Ocicats are very loving and always enjoy human company, but they are not clingy or overly demanding. However, they may get bored and 'naughty' if left on their own often or for extended periods and act out as a result.

Agile, energetic, and athletic, the Ocicat loves hunting games and is capable of extraordinary leaps and agility. They can often be found in high places such as bookshelves or the tops of refrigerators.

Appearance

The most striking features of this breed are the spotted coat and 'wild cat' look. Ocicats are medium to large in size and weigh 6 to 15 lbs. or 2.75 to 6.8 kg. Females weigh less than males. They are muscular and athletic yet graceful in overall build and appearance. The legs match the body in that they are muscular and strong. The paws are oval-shaped and powerful. The Ocicat's tail is long and often has a dark tip.

Their heads are wedge-shaped but longer than they are wide. The face has strong features: a fairly short but broad nose, firm chin and jaw, pronounced cheekbones, and large almond-shaped eyes. Their eyes are especially noticeable thanks to the dark fur that rims them, and they come in every possible color with the exception of blue. The large ears are tilted, have rounded tips, and some cats have vertical tufts of fur on the tips. There is a pronounced "M" marking on the forehead.

Although these cats have been bred for their spots, the Ocicat also comes in other patterns: classic tabby, solid, ticked, and pointed. The spotted coat comes in 12 recognized colors: tawny, fawn, chocolate, cinnamon, blue, lavender, chocolate-silver, cinnamon-silver, blue-silver, ebony-silver, fawn-silver, and lavender-silver.

Regardless of what color the coat is, it features dark thumbprint-shaped spots on a light background. The Ocicat has what is known as an agouti coat. In other words, each individual hair has several bands of color on it. Spots form where the bands of color meet.

The arrangement of the spots is complex. Rows of round spots run along the spine from the shoulder blades to the base of the tail. Spots are scattered across the shoulders and the hindquarters. They also extend down the legs with rings of spots encircling the legs and a string of spots around the neck.

The thumbprint-shaped, large spots are also scattered on the cat's shoulders, sides, and tummy. The markings on the tail look more like horizontal bands and they sometimes alternate with spots. The spots on the shoulders and neck are smaller than the others.

Needs of the breed

The Ocicat's coat is very easy to groom and can be easily kept looking its best by brushing it once a week to remove dead or loose hair.

These cats need space, exercise, and stimulation. If they don't have these things, they may act out or up. If they are not trained when they are kittens, they can be a bit of a handful because they are agile, intelligent, and very determined.

Health

Other than a higher than average tendency to develop gingivitis or gum disease, this breed is not susceptible to any specific genetic conditions or defects.

The Ocicat is a healthy robust breed with a life expectancy of between 12 and 16 years.

Pros and cons

These are loving, loyal, playful, and affectionate cats. They are not clingy or demanding, but because they are a very active breed, they require a lot of space and plenty of toys and diversions to keep them occupied.

They are not a good choice for first-time cat owners or older people and are better suited to more active families with children and / or pets.

Ocicats produce as much Fel d1 protein as any other breed. However, they don't shed very much. As with any breed, though, an allergy sufferer must be exposed to a cat to assess reaction before taking it home.

Price range

At time of writing, the price range for an Ocicat was $300 to $900 or £190 to £580.

The Burmese

History of the breed

The Burmese's ancestors are the Siamese and the "copper cat" of Burma. There are two slightly different versions of how the first Burmese, named Wong Mau, arrived in America. The first version is that Wong Mau was brought to America by a sailor who sold her to Dr. Joseph Thompson. Alternatively, Dr. Thompson himself brought the cat back from a trip to Burma (now Myanmar).

In either event, Wong Mau was probably the natural result of mating between a free-roaming Siamese and a solid-colored Burmese cat. Dr. Thompson bred Wong Mau to Tai Mau, a seal-point Siamese, in 1930. At the same time, breeders Billie Gerst and Virginia Cobb were working to produce kittens with brown, beige, and pointed coats. They also managed to breed for a unique solid brown coat which they called Sable. These various breeders were assisted by Clyde Keeler, who was a geneticist who confirmed the discovery of the Burmese gene. The paper Keeler produced in 1943 helped to establish these cats as a distinct breed.

The Cat Fanciers Association (CFA) registered the Burmese in 1936 but suspended registrations in 1947 because breeders were still using Siamese in their breeding programs. However, registrations were resumed in 1953 after this practice was stopped. The CFA recognizes Sable (dark brown), Champagne (beige), Blue (a medium grey), and Platinum (pale grey).

Breed's temperament

The Burmese is a sociable, playful, adventurous, very loving, single-minded, intelligent, and athletic cat that loves to be involved in everything. They are ideal pets for active homes where there are children and/or cat-friendly dogs.

They are chatty cats with deep, rumbling, soft voices that can become a little more strident if the cat is being ignored. They are skilled at opening doors, and some owners resort to fitting handles upside down to keep their Burmese in or out of rooms.

The Burmese loves games and is fascinated by anything that moves or can be moved. They play fetch with great enthusiasm and are strong jumpers and have been found perched on top of doors and furniture. A handy shoulder or head makes a fun place to nap or way to travel around the house.

This breed is strong-willed and determined, so unless it's acceptable if the home is run by the Burmese and not the human occupants, these cats need to be trained when they are still young.

It is also a very loving breed. These cats will greet their owner on his or her return, follow their person around, 'assist' with tasks and chores, comfort an owner who is sick or sad, and take enthusiastic part in all that happens in the home. Any opportunity for a cuddle and petting will be taken with great and purring enthusiasm.

Appearance

The Burmese is a strong, athletic, and elegant cat that is surprisingly heavy for its size. Because of this, and their very soft coats, these cats are often unflatteringly described as "bricks wrapped in silk." The average weight is 8 - 12 lbs. (4 - 6 kg) with females weighing less than males.

The Burmese is a compact cat with a small, round head and wide-set, large, yellow or gold expressive eyes. There are in fact two body shapes for this breed. The traditional or British type is a more slender, long-bodied cat with a medium length tail, long legs, and oval paws.

These Burmese have a wedge-shaped head, large pointed ears, almond-shaped eyes, and tapering muzzle. The contemporary or American Burmese is much stockier. They have a much broader head, a shorter and flatter muzzle, round eyes, and wider-based ears. Their tail and legs are medium in length, and the paws are rounded rather than oval.

Their coats are short and close-lying and have a very silky texture. The Burmese has a fine, close, even, and glossy coat with a silky or satin-like texture.

The 10 main colors that are recognized by cat associations in the UK and Europe are: brown, brown tortie, chocolate, chocolate tortie, blue, blue tortie, lilac, lilac tortie, cream, and red. In America, only brown (sable), blue, champagne (chocolate), and platinum (lilac) are accepted.

Needs of the breed

The primary requirements of a Burmese are company, love, affection, playtime, and to be part of their owner's life. Games and toys are no substitute for human companionship when it comes to these cats.

If a cat owner works or is away from home for extended hours, it is very important to buy two Burmese kittens, preferably siblings that are from the same litter. Without either human or feline company, these cats become unhappy, even depressed, and can be destructive.

Grooming requirements are minimal. Some recommend a weekly brush while other Burmese owners say that a daily petting is sufficient to keep the coat healthy and free of loose hairs.

Health

These cats are healthy and no more prone to genetic conditions than any other robust breed. The only susceptibility they have is that like many cats, they have a tendency to develop gingivitis or gum disease without correct dental care.

In addition, as with the Rex breeds, the Burmese has a slight tendency to react badly to anesthetics. Milder forms of anesthesia are therefore recommended.

The average life expectancy for a Burmese is 15 years.

Pros and cons

The Burmese is not the right cat for people who want a quiet, docile cat that is independent. They must have company and affection or they become very unhappy and even destructive. However, for those who want a doting, loyal, active, affectionate, and interactive cat, the Burmese is perfect! Also, thanks to the nature of their coat, they require minimal grooming.

A word of warning though their sweet, outgoing, trusting, and fearless natures mean they should be indoor cats as these qualities can get them into dangerous situations.

Burmese produce as much Fel d1 protein as other breeds, but shedding is minimal. As with any breed, though, an allergy sufferer must be exposed to a cat to assess reaction before taking it home.

Price range

At time of writing, the price range for a Burmese was $500 to $800 or £320 to £510.

The Color-point Shorthair

History of the breed

The Color-point Shorthair is yet another breed that was derived from crossing the Siamese with other breeds. Some cat registries and individuals still believe that the Color-point Shorthair is a Siamese hybrid, not a separate breed.

Formal breeding programs were carried out in both America and the UK during the 1940s. Some breeders used crossings between the Siamese, the red domestic shorthair, and the Abyssinian. Other breeding programs used the Siamese and the American Shorthair.

The aim of all the Color-point Shorthair breeding efforts and programs was to produce a breed that had the build and body shape of the Siamese but a much wider range of pointed colors. Of the various colors, red was particularly desirable.

The early years of the breed's development were far from smooth. At times, the desired colors were produced in litters of kittens, but the Siamese body shape was lost in the process. To remedy this problem, the offspring were crossed back to Siamese to regain both body shape and personality. These efforts paid off because now the breed has the Siamese body and head shape and is found in 16 point colors.

In 1964, the Cat Fancier's Association recognized the red and cream pointed Color-point Shorthair. The tortie and lynx (tabby) points were also admitted in 1969. However, the American Cat Fanciers Association (AFCA) and The International Cat Association (TICA) only recognize the Color-point Shorthair as a type of Siamese. In other words, the Cat Fanciers' Association is still the only registry that acknowledges these cats as a separate and standalone breed.

Breed's temperament

The Siamese temperament is fairly strong in the Color-point Shorthair: intelligent, very chatty, loving, sociable, loyal, sensitive to the mood of their owners, playful, and demanding. These cats get along very well with adults and children, other cats, and even with cat-friendly dogs. They not only enjoy company and interaction; they need it.

If a Color-point Shorthair is not getting the attention or levels of interaction it wants, it will use its loud voice to indicate its unhappiness and lodge a complaint. There have been studies done that indicate that this breed produces more than 100 different sounds. This means it has the largest vocabulary of any breed. They enjoy having conversations with their owners too.

Because these cats are both very intelligent and extremely active, they need playtime and exercise. Puzzle and teaser toys are the best choice for the Color-point Shorthair. Ideally, one should supply toys and an animal companion if the human companion will be out for extended periods. Interaction is essential for this breed. They will follow their owner around and 'help' with tasks or at least offer advice.

In addition, they can problem-solve and have no difficulty opening doors or drawers. Their agility and athleticism helps with these activities too. They enjoy climbing into and onto things and exploring areas in their home. If they find something interesting, they will tell their owner.

These cats are very loving and loyal but do demand time and an equal measure of affection and time from their owner.

Appearance

The looks of the Color-point Shorthair are as similar to the Siamese as their temperament is. If one compared a Siamese and a Color-point Shorthair by feel only, it would be very hard to tell them apart. These are elegant, medium-sized cats that weigh on average 5 to 10 lbs. or 2.25 to 4.5 kg.

The body is long, well-muscled, and lean. Their bones are fine, which results in slim, long, and delicate-looking legs. The hind legs are a little longer than the front ones. The breed's paws are oval and neat.

The head is the typical Siamese-like wedge shape with striking medium-sized, almond-shaped, slanting eyes and very large, flared ears that are triangular in shape. Eye color is usually a shade of blue, and odd eyes can also occur. The tail is long and thin and tapers to a point.

The only way in which the Siamese and Color-point Shorthair are materially different is in terms of color. The range of coat point colors found include red, tortie, cream, and combinations of these three.

Needs of the breed

The Color-point Shorthair needs company, attention, activity, stimulation, and more attention. If it doesn't get enough, it will object very loudly and incessantly.

These cats require minimal grooming; a weekly or twice weekly brush is more than adequate to remove loose or dead hair and ensure coat health. A bath should not be necessary.

As with all cats, their nails need clipping from time to time, and their teeth must be cleaned daily or at least weekly to prevent periodontal or gum disease.

Health

This breed is generally healthy and not known to be susceptible to any specific genetic illnesses or defects. The only issue, thanks to the Siamese heritage, is crossed or partially crossed eyes.

With the correct nutrition and care, the Color-point Shorthair will live for 12 to 17 years.

Pros and cons

For some owners, the fact that these cats are active, playful, interactive, and highly vocal will be an advantage. For others, the demanding, even clingy, nature and loud conversation of the Color-point Shorthair is a definite disadvantage. Certainly, their loving and loyal natures will appeal to everyone.

These cats can also be highly-strung and easily startled. They seldom adapt well or easily to change and don't usually travel well.

Price range

At time of writing, the price range for a Color-point Shorthair was $400 to $700 or £260 to £450.

The Siamese

History of the breed

The Siamese is arguably the most recognizable cat breed in the world, even amongst people who are not cat lovers. This breed can be traced back to 14th century Siam, known today as Thailand. These elegant and distinctive cats were greatly prized and were given as gifts to visiting dignitaries by the royal family of Siam.

Siamese were seen in America and Europe for the first time in the late 1800s. The first one arrived in America in 1878, and it was a gift to President Hayes from the American Consul based in Bangkok. The UK's first breeding pair, Mia and Pho, arrived in 1884 when the British Consul-General brought them back to England as a gift for his sister, Lilian Jane Veley. She went on to breed Siamese and co-found the Siamese Cat Club. Unfortunately, all three of the kittens she exhibited died. Another breeding pair, along with their offspring, was imported into the UK in 1886. This small group of cats was added to over several years.

These early Siamese looked very different to the Siamese we are accustomed today because they were medium-sized and muscular cats. They were graceful and had long bodies, moderately wedge-shaped heads, and comparatively large ears. By the 1950s and 1960s, these cats, which were originally unattractive and 'unnatural,' had gained in popularity. However, judges at shows and cat owners began to prefer the Siamese that were more slender. Breeding efforts therefore began to focus on producing long, narrow, fine-boned cats that had slim legs and a thin tail.

By the mid-1980s, the earlier, less slender Siamese had disappeared altogether from cat shows. However, breeders in the UK continue to produce the traditional and less elongated cats.

The breed has also given rise to several others or been used to create them. These breeds include the various Oriental breeds (Balinese, Javanese, Color-point, Oriental Longhair, and Oriental Shorthair), the Burmese, Tonkinese, Ocicat, Snowshoe, and the Korat.

Breed's temperament

Highly intelligent, playful well into adulthood, energetic, and agile, the Siamese can be trained to respond to commands and perform tricks. They also do very well with agility training and competitions. They are very social and enjoy the company of other cats, especially Siamese, but need human companionship.

They are also very dependent on their owners. Siamese crave active involvement in the life of their owner or human family and rely on companionship from their owner. Without it, these cats become unhappy, depressed, and sometimes destructive. This makes them a bad choice for people who are away from home often or for extended periods. Siamese can be unpredictable and require a great deal of affection in order to develop a close relationship with their human companions.

These cats are also extremely talkative and love to communicate with their people. Their voices are loud and raspy, and they have a large vocabulary. Some say their cries sound like those of a human baby. If these cats are ignored, they will demand attention in a very strident fashion that is impossible to ignore.

These cats need to be handled carefully when they are kittens and socialized with care. When they are shown love, patience, and care, they make wonderfully loving and loyal companions.

Appearance

The modern Siamese has a svelte, elongated, muscular body. Some cat associations describe the standard body shape as "tubular." Despite the fact that these cats are well-muscled, they look fairly delicate. It comes as a surprise that the average adult weight is 6 to 14 pounds or 2.7 to 6.35 kg.

The body is supported by legs that are slim and long. The hind legs are slightly longer than the front legs. The paws of the Siamese are small, dainty, and oval in shape rather than round. Their tails are long, thin, and whip-like and taper to a point.

The head is long and distinctly wedge-shaped. The very large ears are triangular with a wide base and pointed tips. The characteristic Siamese eyes are a piercing blue, almond-shaped, and medium in size. Some cats still have slightly crossed eyes, although crossed eyes are increasingly rare. There are also Siamese that have odd eyes.

The short coat contains a mutated enzyme in its pigment. Interestingly, the color is limited to the point areas because this enzyme is temperature-controlled: it creates areas of darker color at the parts of the body that are farthest away from the heart and lungs.

This also explains why Siamese kittens are born white. The warmth of their mother's body prevents the color forming, and the Siamese develops its point color as it grows.

It is this enzyme that is responsible for the cream color of the torso and the darker points (face, ears, tail, and toes). In terms of colors, the Cat Fanciers Association (CFA) recognizes the four traditional colors: seal (black), chocolate (brown), blue (grey dilution of seal), and lilac (dilution of the chocolate). The International Cat Association (TICA) also allows lynx and tortoiseshell.

Needs of the breed

The Siamese needs company, attention, activity, stimulation, and more attention. If it doesn't get enough, it will object very loudly and incessantly.

These cats require minimal grooming; a weekly or twice weekly brush is more than adequate to remove loose or dead hair and ensure coat health. A bath should not be necessary.

As with all cats, their nails need clipping from time to time, and their teeth must be cleaned daily or at least weekly to prevent periodontal or gum disease.

Health

The Siamese is generally speaking a healthy and robust breed. However, these cats can be genetically predisposed to gingivitis or gum disease and to amyloidosis, which destroys the liver.

With amyloidosis, a fibrous protein called amyloid is deposited in the liver. These deposits disrupt the normal functioning of the organ. There is no cure for amyloidosis, but supportive care is very helpful.

Good, professional breeding practices have largely bred out the cross-eyed and kinked tail tendencies, although both can still occur. Neither is harmful to the cat's overall well-being.

With the correct nutrition and care, the Siamese will live for 14 to 18 years.

Pros and cons

For some owners, the fact that these cats are active, playful, interactive, and highly vocal will be an advantage. For others, the demanding, clingy nature, and loud conversation of the Siamese are a disadvantage. Certainly, their loving and loyal natures will appeal to everyone.

These cats can also be highly-strung and easily startled. They seldom adapt well or easily to change and don't usually travel well.

Price range

At time of writing, the price range for a Siamese was $400 to $600 or £260 to £380.

The Sphynx

History of the breed

The Sphynx traces its origins back in part to a litter of shorthaired cats born in 1966 in Toronto, Canada. Amongst this litter was a single, hairless male kitten that was named Prune. When he was old enough, he was mated with his mother who subsequently produced a second generation of hairless kittens.

The 1970s saw two sets of hairless cats emerge in the North Americas. There were three cats in Toronto and two in Minnesota. These cats formed the gene pool out of which it was hoped a new breed could be developed. The breeding program was led by a man by the name of Mr. Bawa, his mother who was a successful Siamese breeder, and a couple by the name of Tenhove. The breed they jointly produced was named "Sphynx" because of its similarity to sculptures of cats found in ancient Egypt.

In the 1970s and the 1980s, the breeding program encountered serious problems. In order to keep breeding lines going, a breeder in the Netherlands, Dr. Hugo Hernandez, outcrossed his female

Sphynx with a Devon-Rex. This was successful, and the 1990s saw a significant increase in the size and strength of the gene pool.

The Cat Fancier's Association (CFA) recognized the breed, but subsequently revoked their decision. It was not until February 1998 that the CFA accepted the Sphynx breed for both competition and registration.

In 1985, The International Cat Association (TICA) registered the breed. The 1990s brought acceptance from the American Association of Cat Fanciers (ACFA) and full status from CFA in 2002.

Breed's temperament

The Sphynx is described as intelligent, inquisitive, entertaining, clownish, athletic, demonstrative and cuddly, loving, sociable, affectionate, playful, mischievous, companionable, sweet-tempered, active, adventurous, loyal, cheeky, and a flirt. In fact, most owners place the words "extremely" or "incredibly" or at the very least "very" in front of each of those adjectives.

Sphynx cats enjoy the company of other cats and cat-friendly dogs, and they will also be friendly to your guests. However, they adore the companionship of their person and will follow him or her around. These cats are always ready for a cuddle or a game, and they hate being on their own. In addition, this is a very chatty or talkative breed, although their voice is not as strident as, for instance, the Siamese's.

They are also very loyal and sensitive to their owner's emotions. Many sources state that the Sphynx is the most intelligent of cat breeds. Their intelligence means that they need a great deal of interaction and stimulation either from their owner or from another cat or both. However, because of their natural curiosity, intelligence, and desire to please, they are easy to train.

They can even be taught to walk on a leash and are happy to go on fairly long walks if accompanied by their owner. In addition to going for walks, a Sphynx will learn to play fetch and do tricks that it finds fun and that it realizes you enjoy, and it will respond to certain voice commands.

Appearance

The Sphynx is a medium-sized, well-muscled cat. The weight range for the breed is 6 to 15lbs or 2.7 to 6.8kg. The males are, as a rule, about 25% larger than the females.

The Sphynx has a wedge-shaped head and very prominent cheekbones. The skin on the face, neck, and elsewhere where it is loose is quite wrinkled. The eyes are lemon-shaped, large, and very expressive. The body and neck are both muscular and medium in length. Their ears are very large and hairless inside.

These cats are barrel-chested and have round tummies that look as though they have just enjoyed a good meal. Their legs are long, slim, and elegant, and the oval paws boast unusually thick pads and long toes. The pads make these cats look as they are walking on air. The tail is thin and whip-like and may have a small tuft of hair in the tip.

The Sphynx may appear to be hairless, but these cats are in fact covered with an extremely fine down. This makes these cats feel like warm and soft chamois leather. While it can be almost impossible to see the very fine fur, the Sphynx can – even for judging purposes – have fine, short hair on the feet, tail, muzzle, ears, and scrotum. Some Sphynx have eyebrows and some whiskers, and others have none at all.

The skin is the color their fur would be if they had any. All the usual cat markings or patterns can be found on Sphynx skin. These cats are therefore found in a wide range of colors: pure white, solid colors such as black, pointed, tabby, and even tortoiseshell. They can have bi-colored or odd eyes. Many Sphynx cats have blue eyes.

Needs of the breed

These medium size cats do not require a great deal of space. They do, however, need company and a great deal of mental stimulation.

They are also, preferably, indoor cats because they are more vulnerable to the sun and sunburn and to potential rashes and so on caused by contact with some plants, grasses etc. They also, understandably, feel the cold far more than most other breeds.

Sphynx cats require thorough and regular grooming. The lack of coat means that the cat's owner must deal with the oils that build up on the skin and the wax, oil, and so on in the ears. A weekly bath is essential to prevent bacterial infections.

As with other cats, nails need trimming and teeth must be cleaned weekly, preferably daily, in order to prevent gum disease.

Health

While they are generally healthy, they do carry the risk of a few conditions that can affect many breeds. These include a heart disease called hypertrophic cardiomyopathy and hereditary myopathy. The latter is, fortunately, increasingly rare.

Hypertrophic cardiomyopathy is a condition that results in an enlarged heart muscle. Although this is a serious and incurable disease, it can be managed and controlled with medication, diet, and by keeping the cat relaxed, at ideal weight, and not exercising it too much. With the right care and an early diagnosis, these cats can live good and happy lives for many years.

Hereditary myopathy is a central nervous illness that affects muscle function and control, rather like cerebral palsy. With this condition, there is no treatment, and only supportive care can be given. The disease is usually stable or slowly progressive. The course of the disease will depend on the severity of the myopathy.

Like most cats, the Sphynx can suffer from gum and tooth problems, but this can usually be avoided with good basic oral hygiene. In addition, these cats are very fond of their food and tend to gain weight unless they are kept on a calorie controlled diet.

If they are taken good care of, the life expectancy of the Sphynx is 12-15 years or more.

Pros and cons

While the Sphynx produces a negligible amount of dander, there will still be some. They produce as much Fel d1 protein as most other breeds. However, this can be controlled by the necessary grooming regimen. For those with cat allergies, the weekly bathing is therefore essential for both them and the cat!

Sphynx cats really do require thorough and regular grooming. The lack of coat means that the oils that build up on the skin and the wax, oil, and so on in the ears must be dealt with. Some people find the grooming too time-consuming, even unpleasant. This should be kept in mind when considering this breed. As with other cats, nails need trimming and teeth must be cleaned regularly to prevent dental and oral health-related problems.

Given the lack of coat, they are more vulnerable to the sun so their exposure to it should be limited as they can get burnt or, worst case scenario, develop skin cancer in later life. This is especially true of Sphynx cats with light pigmentation in their skins.

Price range

At time of writing, the price range for a Sphynx was $1200 to $1800 or £770 to £1155.

Summary of some of the main features and characteristics of the 14 hypoallergenic cats breeds

Having some detailed information on the various hypoallergenic breeds is useful, but it can also be a little overwhelming. The following list aims to help focus on the primary features or characteristics of these cats. For example, if one wants a loving, intelligent cat that is easy to groom and not demanding or 'loud,' then the Siberian is one of the breeds that would be suitable.

Longhaired:

Siberian
Balinese
LaPerm

Medium length coat:

Javanese

Shorthaired:

Bengal
Devon Rex
Oriental Shorthair
Russian Blue
Ocicat
Burmese
Color-point Shorthair
Siamese

Undercoat only:

Cornish Rex

Hairless:

Sphynx

Affectionate and loving:

Siberian
Balinese
Javanese
Bengal
Cornish Rex
Devon Rex
LaPerm
Oriental Shorthair
Russian Blue
Ocicat
Burmese
Color-point Shorthair
Siamese
Sphynx

Active and athletic:

Siberian
Balinese
Javanese
Bengal
Cornish Rex
Devon Rex
LaPerm
Oriental Shorthair
Ocicat
Burmese
Color-point Shorthair
Siamese
Sphynx

Playful and curious:

Siberian
Balinese
Javanese

Bengal
Cornish Rex
Devon Rex
LaPerm
Oriental Shorthair
Russian Blue
Ocicat
Burmese
Color-point Shorthair
Siamese
Sphynx

Intelligent and easy to train:

Siberian
Balinese
Javanese
Bengal
Cornish Rex
Devon Rex
LaPerm
Oriental
Shorthair
Russian Blue
Ocicat
Burmese
Color-point Shorthair
Siamese
Sphynx

Good with other animals:

Siberian
Balinese
Javanese
Bengal
Cornish Rex
Devon Rex

LaPerm
Oriental Shorthair
Ocicat
Color-point Shorthair
Sphynx

Good with children:

Siberian
Balinese
Javanese
Bengal
Cornish Rex
Devon Rex
LaPerm
Oriental Shorthair
Russian Blue
Color-point Shorthair
Sphynx

Easy-going and relaxed:

Siberian
Devon Rex
Sphynx

Enjoy water:

Siberian
Bengal

Low grooming needs:

Siberian
Balinese
Javanese
Bengal
Cornish Rex
Devon Rex

LaPerm
Oriental Shorthair
Russian Blue
Ocicat
Burmese
Color-point Shorthair
Siamese

High grooming needs:

Sphynx

Demanding:

Balinese
Javanese
Bengal
Devon Rex
Oriental Shorthair
Burmese
Color-point Shorthair
Siamese
Sphynx

Very talkative:

Balinese
Javanese
Bengal
Cornish Rex
Oriental Shorthair
Color-point Shorthair
Siamese
Sphynx

Loud voice:

Bengal
Oriental Shorthair

Ocicat
Burmese
Color-point Shorthair
Siamese
Sphynx

Quiet voice:

Siberian
Cornish Rex
Devon Rex
LaPerm
Russian Blue

Able to entertain themselves:

Siberian
Devon Rex
LaPerm
Russian Blue

CHAPTER 4: FIGHTING ALLERGENS

While there are the 14 breeds that present less of a problem for allergy sufferers, it must be remembered that there is no such thing as a non-allergenic cat. Certain people will react badly to all cats.

It may be the dander (loose hair and dead skin cells) that bothers them or the Fel d1 protein (found in saliva and therefore on the fur) or both. Both allergens may cause the all-too-familiar allergy symptoms such as itching, sneezing, red and irritated eyes, or even more serious symptoms such as breathing problems.

All allergy sufferers are different, which is why it is so important that they are exposed to a cat for a few hours before deciding whether or not it is the hypoallergenic breed that is right for them. An allergy sufferer must therefore arrange with the breeder to have this exposure time as part of the decision-making process.

In addition to choosing a breed that is optimally hypoallergenic for the sufferer, there are also ways one can reduce the presence of allergens both on the cat and in the home generally.

On your cat

1. **Brushing**:

   The easiest way to reduce allergens on and from a cat is with regular grooming. If you have a family member who is not allergic to cats, he or she should be the one to do the grooming.

   It may be that a weekly brushing is not enough to control the presence of loose hair and dander. In this case, daily brushing might be a good option. Brushing is effective because it removes dead or loose hair, dust, dried skin cells, and any outdoor allergens such as pollen that a cat's coat may have come into contact with.

Although some cats love the attention and the sensation of being brushed, others don't. It is therefore important to get a cat used to being brushed when it is young.

Once the brushing has been done, the hair should be removed from the brush or comb, which should then also be rinsed or washed. The hair removed from the brush or comb should be thrown away outside.

2. **Bathing**:

The second way to control allergens produced by a cat is by bathing it. The Sphynx must be bathed once a week anyway, but giving other breeds a bath every week or two weeks can help to reduce dander and control Fel d1. Of course, these substances build up again in between baths.

There are a few breeds that enjoy water, but most cats hate it. Bathing a cat is therefore very stressful for the cat and can be very painful for the person trying to manage and wash a writhing, hissing, wet, and furious cat. As with brushing, introducing baths when a cat is very young can help to get them used to bathing even if they never enjoy it.

It is also essential to use a cat shampoo as others can cause skin conditions such as dry skin or dandruff and irritations. There are also shampoos specifically for the purpose of reducing allergens.

One can either select an appropriate cat shampoo from a pet store or one could ask the breeder or a vet's advice on which one would be best at reducing allergens and for the breed of the specific cat.

In your home

There are a number of actions one can take to make a home less allergenic. Preferably, the following tasks should be performed by members of the household who are not allergic to cats:

- ➢ Don't allow the cat or cats to go into the bedroom of the person with allergies. By keeping the cat out of the room and off the bed, one goes a long way to preventing dander and Fel d1 getting onto surfaces and bedding.

- ➢ Keep cats out of rooms with carpets or rugs or at least off carpets or rugs as they trap dander. This is not very easy with adult cats, but if one trains a cat not to lie on soft surfaces or furnishings, except its own bedding, when it is young, it should not be problematic.

- ➢ Keep cats off upholstered furniture because the fabric also traps dander. Again, training a cat not to lie on soft surfaces or furnishings, except its own bedding, when it is young is the best way to achieve this.

- ➢ Use allergen resistant bedding, which does not attract or hold dander that drifts into the bedroom. One can find this type of bedding from good retail stores or purchase it online.

  It's important to remember that having allergen resistant bedding does not mean that it's then alright to allow a cat onto an allergy sufferer's bed.

- ➢ Use anti-allergen sprays in the home. They are considered to be an easy and fairly effective way to deactivate airborne allergens, including those produced by cats. Some of these sprays are plant-based and are therefore non-toxic and will not add to the allergens in the home by introducing chemicals. They can safely be used around children too.

➢ Vacuum all indoor surfaces that cats come into contact with daily. This may sound onerous but can make a very marked difference as it will remove any dander and loose hair that carries Fel d1.

➢ Wash cat bedding regularly and air it in between washes. If a cat is spending a lot of time grooming and sleeping on its bedding, then a great deal of loose hair, dander, and Fel d1 will end up on and in the bedding. This must be removed before it is blown into the home and settles on other surfaces or is inhaled by the person battling allergies.

➢ Replace wall-to-wall or fitted carpets with allergy resistant carpeting or with wooden or tile flooring as they don't trap dander and are easier to clean. Suppliers and fitters of these types of floor coverings are easy to locate.

It's important to remember that having allergen resistant carpets or hard flooring does not mean that it's then alright to allow a cat onto an allergy sufferer's bed.

➢ Invest in a high-efficiency particulate air (HEPA) filter or double bag vacuum cleaner. These machines are reportedly far more effective and suck up 99.7% of small particles. This effectiveness does mean that they can be more costly than ordinary vacuum cleaners. They will collect pet hair and dander with ease.

The filters should, on average, be replaced with a new one every six months. However, one should check the manual because each vacuum cleaner is different.

➢ One should be careful about when one does the vacuuming. Firstly, vacuum and dust when the allergy-sufferer is not at home. In addition, even if one is using a high-efficiency particulate air (HEPA) machine, one shouldn't vacuum right before bed as the process does stir up a little dander, dust, etc. Finally, don't vacuum when children are present as they are closer to the ground and therefore more likely to inhale the particles that circulate.

➢ Empty vacuum cleaners, vacuum cleaner bags, or filters outside and away from open house doors and windows so that no substances in the bag blow or drift back into the home as this entirely defeats the purpose of vacuuming.

➢ Close the air registers or grilles in forced-air heating and air conditioning units as it should reduce the amount of dander circulating through the home. It is also very important to have these grilles or registers cleaned regularly as, even when closed, they will accumulate particles that can be problematic for the allergy sufferer.

➢ Replace the filter in the furnace or air conditioner with a high-efficiency particulate air (HEPA) filter. This will prevent dander being circulated through the house. These filters should, on average, be replaced with a new one every six months. However, one should check the manual as it can vary.

➢ Purchase and use an air purifier or air cleaner that will help to remove allergens from the environment. The most important components of this type of machine are its air filters. Indeed, most air purifiers and air cleaners contain at least two air filters.

Some of these machines use three or four different types of air filters. There are numerous types of filters, and they include activated carbon, ion and ozone generators, electrostatic precipitators, or a mixture of them.

One can also select from a portable air purifier, a whole-house air cleaner, or a whole-house air filter. A salesperson at a reputable retailer or installer will be able to offer advice on the most suitable type.

➢ Open doors and windows whenever the weather permits so that there is cross-ventilation that removes allergens floating in the air. Naturally, this is not advisable if the allergy sufferer also has a problem with allergens found outside, such as pollen, spores, dust, or soil, because these particles may enter the house.

CHAPTER 5: FREQUENTLY ASKED QUESTIONS

What Causes Cat Allergies?

Pet allergies are common with cats being greater culprits than dogs. Most people think it is the cat's fur or hair that causes the problem. However, this is not accurate.

The allergens are dander (a mixture of dead hair, skin cells, dust, saliva) that is deposited on surfaces or drifts around in the air and—the main culprit—the protein known as Fel d1 that is found in the cat's saliva and urine. Given that cats groom themselves by licking, these proteins are found on their coats and, in small quantities, in dander.

The other possibility is that a person is not actually allergic to cats at all but reacts to substances such as pollen, dust, or mold that the cat comes into contact with and then brings into the house with them.

People who suffer from allergies have oversensitive immune systems. When their bodies encounter substances, including totally harmless ones like cat dander, they overreact and behave as though they are dangerous invading organisms like bacteria or a virus. The body then attacks the invaders. Allergies are in fact the side-effects of the body's overzealous reaction.

What Are the Symptoms of Cat Allergies?

Symptoms of an allergic reaction to a cat vary from person to person. However, there are several that are often found or are more common than others. These include:

- Sneezing

- Red and / or itchy eyes
- Coughing
- Running or blocked nose
- Wheezing
- Itchy nose
- Rash on the face and/or chest
- Redness or itching where the skin has been in contact with the cat.

These can also be a reaction to other allergens, not necessarily a cat.

How Do I Know if I Have a Cat Allergy?

Some people come into contact with a cat, experience allergy-like symptoms, and assume the cat is the cause. This is not always the case. One way to assess this is by going to your doctor for skin or blood tests. Alternatively, if the cat is removed and the symptoms clear quickly and totally, it is pretty obvious that the cat was the allergen.

How Are Cat Allergies Treated?

Cat allergies are usually controlled with the same range of remedies and drugs or medications as other types of allergies. Many of these can be bought over the counter and don't need a doctor's prescription. For example:

- Antihistamines: there is a very wide range of these products available. They come in tablet and nasal spray forms.

- Decongestants: there are numerous products in this category too, and their function is to ease the congestion in the nose and sinuses that is experienced by some allergy sufferers.

For more marked allergic reactions, doctors might prescribe or recommend nasal sprays that contain steroids that will help with breathing problems. Some doctors might suggest that a patient have allergy shots, although these are not always effective and a full course of treatment can extend over years.

CHAPTER 6: USEFUL RESOURCES

Allergy resources

There are numerous resources available for those who suffer from allergies or have a family member who does.

Resources can be found online, at clinics or hospitals, doctor's rooms, veterinarian practices, community centers, etc. While some of these resources are local or regional, others are global. No matter where one is, help and information can be found.

North America

American Board of Allergy and Immunology: abai.org

The American Board of Allergy and Immunology (ABAI) is a non-profit organization that is committed to working to "maintain the highest educational and clinical standards in the specialty of allergy/immunology."

ABAI provides information about specialist certification for the benefit of the public, government, and professionals.

American Academy of Allergy, Asthma and Immunology: aaai.org

The American Academy of Allergy, Asthma & Immunology (AAAAI) is a professional organization that operates in the United States, Canada, and 72 other countries. Their members include allergists / immunologists, medical specialists, and allied health and related healthcare professionals. All the members have a special interest in the research and treatment of allergic and immunologic diseases.

Their website provides various useful resources and links.

Allergy and Asthma Network Mothers of Asthmatics: aanma.org

Allergy & Asthma Network is, according to their website, a "nonprofit family health organization whose mission is to end needless suffering and death due to asthma, allergies and related conditions through education, advocacy and outreach."

They offer a one-stop, family-to-family support forum and also offer a network magazine and monthly e-newsletter for those who have children who suffer from allergies.

Asthma & Allergy Foundation of America: aafa.org

The Asthma and Allergy Foundation of America (AAFA) is a not-for-profit organization for people with allergies and asthma. They state that they are in fact the oldest such group in the world. Their aim is to improve the quality of life for people with allergies and asthma "through education, advocacy and research."

The organization has a large national network that provides help and support to sufferers. They state that they "provide online access to… reliable, validated asthma and allergy information and tools to families, patients, parents, [and] healthcare providers."

UK

Allergy UK: allergyuk.org

Allergy UK is the trading name of the British Allergy Foundation. The organization is also a non-profit entity. It offers a dedicated helpline, a wide range of online resources and links, an online forum for allergy sufferers and their family members, and a national support network.

Other regions and countries

Anaphylaxis Australia: allergyfacts.org.au

Allergy & Anaphylaxis Australia (A&AA) is a not for profit organization. Its aims are to raise awareness of allergies by sharing information and through education, advocacy, research, guidance, and support.

Their website contains useful information and also offers an online store for various items including books.

Suggested books

There are two useful books on the subject of allergies that are available through Allergy UK (allergyuk.org):

1. "Allergies: Answers at Your Fingertips" by Dr. Jo Clough: This book answers more than 300 questions about allergies and is a very handy FAQ and Q&A guide to have.

2. "Allergies—A Parent's Guide" by Victoria Goldman: This book is aimed at parents who need an accessible book that contains practical advice on preventing allergies and managing symptoms.

There are numerous other books on the subject available from stores and online retailers like Amazon, such as, "Allergy-free Living" by Peter Howarth. This particular book is a guide to creating an allergen-free and healthy home environment. It also provides practical tips and advice.

Resources for cat owners

American Association of Feline Practitioners: catvets.com/cat-owners/brochures

While this association is aimed primarily at veterinarians and other animal health care practitioners, their website has a tab for "Cat Owners" where a large number of useful resources including brochures and booklets can be found and downloaded.

Sheltering Hands: shelteringhands.com/Resources-for-cat-owners.html

This website is designed for cat owners and lovers. It provides a very wide range of resources including booklets and articles that are available as pdf files for downloading and printing. This website is updated frequently and is easy to navigate.

And finally, keep in mind that there are other resources close at hand when it comes to information you need about your individual cat or the breed that it belongs to:

- ➤ The breeder that you bought your kitten from will have sound knowledge of cats generally and of the breed they work with especially. It's a good idea to obtain all the information that you can when you first buy your cat. It is not unusual, however, that additional information is needed once the cat is in your home and you are spending time together. Most breeders have their cat's interests at heart, even after a sale, and are therefore happy to answer questions at a later stage or refer you to the right person or organization.

- ➤ Your cat's veterinarian is of course a mine of information in relation to cats in general and your cat in particular. He or she can also recommend other useful resources or refer you to individuals and organizations that will be able to assist you. Often the staff members at a vet's rooms or animal clinics are also very helpful and approachable. Many of these establishments also have stands of brochures and leaflets in their waiting rooms that contain useful and or interesting information.

➢ Most recognized or accepted breeds have official societies or clubs that offer cat owners and potential cat owners information on that specific breed. An internet search should help you find these without any difficulty.

➢ A less formal resource is blogs and forums for cat owners. Some are general sites for cat owners and lovers and others are breed-specific. These sites can be a lot of fun and sources of very good information. However, one does need to keep in mind that the blogs and forum postings usually express the views of other cat owners. This means that the quality or reliability of the information will vary. One needs to use one's judgment to assess this.

Lightning Source UK Ltd.
Milton Keynes UK
UKHW020309041222
413325UK00010B/624